Amazing Animals

Venomous Snakes

Fractions and Decimals

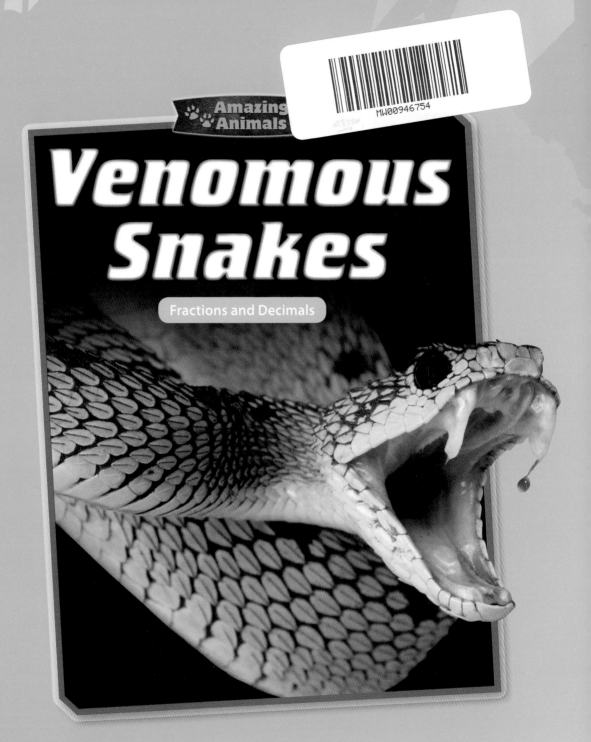

Noelle Hoffmeister, M.A.

Consultants

Michele Ogden, Ed.D
Principal
Irvine Unified School District

Colleen Pollitt, M.A.Ed.
Math Support Teacher
Howard County Public Schools

Publishing Credits

Rachelle Cracchiolo, M.S.Ed., *Publisher*
Conni Medina, M.A.Ed., *Managing Editor*
Dona Herweck Rice, *Series Developer*
Emily R. Smith, M.A.Ed., *Series Developer*
Diana Kenney, M.A.Ed., NBCT, *Content Director*
Stacy Monsman, M.A., *Editor*
Kevin Panter, *Graphic Designer*

Image Credits: p.6 Illustration by Timothy J. Bradley;
p.10–11 Avalon/Photoshot License/ Alamy Stock Photo; p.16 (bottom)
RosalreneBetancourt 6/ Alamy Stock Photo; p.20 (bottom) ANT Photo Library/
Science Source; p.26 travelib sulawesi/Alamy Stock Photo; p.27 RIA Novosti/
Sputnik/Science Source; p.28 Arterra Picture Library/Alamy Stock Photo; all other
images from iStock and/or Shutterstock.

Library of Congress Cataloging-in-Publication Data

Names: Hoffmeister, Noelle, author.
Title: Venomous snakes : fractions and decimals / Noelle Hoffmeister, M.A.
Description: Huntington Beach, CA : Teacher Created Materials, [2018] |
   Series: Amazing animals | Audience: Grade 4 to 6. | Includes index.
Identifiers: LCCN 2017012136 (print) | LCCN 2017014384 (ebook) | ISBN
   9781480759398 (eBook) | ISBN 9781425855574 (paperback)
Subjects: LCSH: Poisonous snakes--Venom--Juvenile literature. | Poisonous
   snakes--Juvenile literature.
Classification: LCC QL666.O6 (ebook) | LCC QL666.O6 H665 2018 (print) | DDC
   597.96/165--dc23
LC record available at https://lccn.loc.gov/2017012136

Teacher Created Materials

5301 Oceanus Drive
Huntington Beach, CA 92649-1030
http://www.tcmpub.com

ISBN 978-1-4258-5557-4
© 2018 Teacher Created Materials, Inc.

Table of Contents

Mysterious Venomous Snakes

Imagine walking through a hot, dry desert in North America. The blazing sun beats down on your body as you walk across the sand. To your left are green cacti covered with spiny needles. To your right, if you look closely, are lizards scurrying across the sand and hiding under rocks for shade. Small birds hop on the sand, chirping and talking to each other. You are grateful to have your water bottle with you on this journey. As you stop to take a drink, you feel the cool liquid on your lips. As you step over a rock, you hear a soft rattle coming from behind you. Immediately, you freeze. You've been warned about this sound. Could it be a **venomous** snake?

Although we don't see them much, it's easy to find venomous snakes. They live on almost every **continent** in the world. Snakes don't need a lot to survive. Their two main necessities are food and warm weather for part of the year. The maps in this book show where different species of venomous snakes live. Take a look. There may be a species near you!

NORTH
ATLANTIC

NORTH
PACIFIC

INDIAN
OCEAN

SOUTH
PACIFIC

SOUTH
ATLANTIC

| | regions where venomous snakes live |

ANTARCTICA

Venomous snakes are any snake species that uses **venom**, or poison, to capture their **prey**. The teeth of these snakes are curved inward to help them hold their **prey** in their mouths. This is one way they've **adapted** over time. Adaptations are slow changes over thousands of years that help living organisms survive.

Most venomous snakes eat small animals, such as rats, mice, lizards, frogs, and birds. They even eat bird eggs. How does a snake capture its meal? First, it bites its prey. As it bites, the snake's venom moves into its hollow, tube-like teeth. The venom in this bite makes its prey stop moving. The venom flows into the body of the prey and **paralyzes** it. The snake is now ready to eat. It swallows its meal whole! Snakes have a separate lower jaw and strong tendons that help them **ingest** large food. The digestive system of snakes is so strong that it can break down eggshells and even bones!

All around the world, venomous snakes are known for their speed, **agility**, and dangerous bites. But, each species has specific features that make them unique.

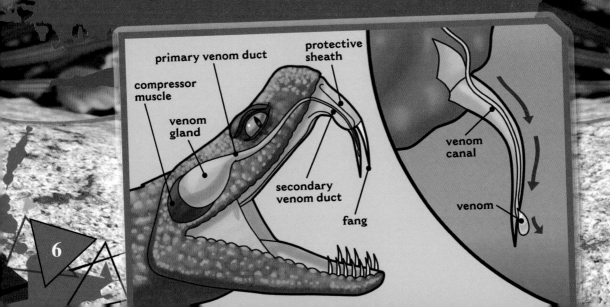

primary venom duct

protective sheath

compressor muscle

venom gland

secondary venom duct

fang

venom canal

venom

A snake releases venom from its sharp, curved fangs.

LET'S EXPLORE MATH

Not all snakes in the world have venom. It is estimated that only $\frac{2}{10}$ of snakes are venomous. Draw the number line shown below and label the missing fractions and decimals. Then, plot a point to show $\frac{2}{10}$.

0.1   0.5   1.0

0   $\frac{1}{10}$ $\frac{5}{10}$ 1

Cunning Cobras

You wouldn't want to run into king cobras in the wild! They are the largest venomous snakes in the world. They can grow up to 18 feet (5 meters) long—the same height as 3 adults standing on top of one another! King cobras can weigh up to 20 pounds (9 kilograms) and can live up to 20 years.

A king cobra may not have a leg to stand on, but that doesn't stop it from standing tall! It has the ability to lift the front third of its body up to 6 ft. (2 m) off the ground!

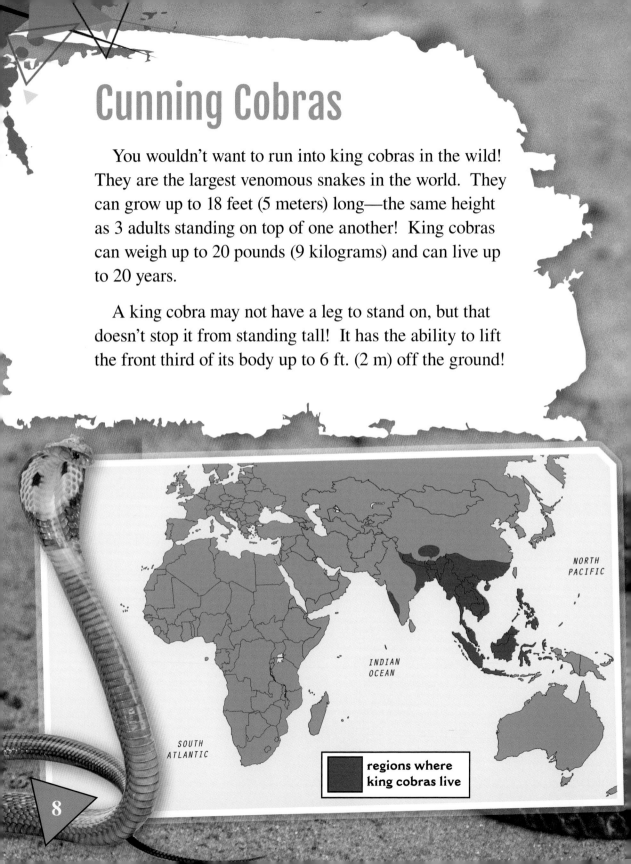

NORTH PACIFIC

INDIAN OCEAN

SOUTH ATLANTIC

regions where king cobras live

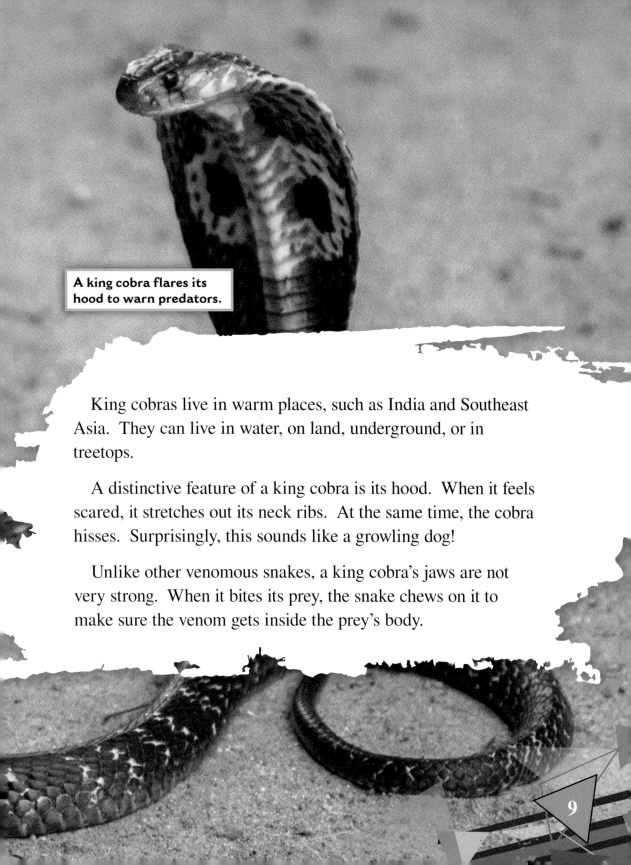

A king cobra flares its hood to warn predators.

King cobras live in warm places, such as India and Southeast Asia. They can live in water, on land, underground, or in treetops.

A distinctive feature of a king cobra is its hood. When it feels scared, it stretches out its neck ribs. At the same time, the cobra hisses. Surprisingly, this sounds like a growling dog!

Unlike other venomous snakes, a king cobra's jaws are not very strong. When it bites its prey, the snake chews on it to make sure the venom gets inside the prey's body.

King cobras are very dangerous. Only $\frac{5}{100}$ of the venom in a king cobra's bite is needed to kill a human. Victims of bites have 30 minutes to get help or they may die.

Even so, king cobras are not only **predators**, but they are also prey! The Indian gray mongoose is a predator of the cobra. Cobras hiss and show their hoods when they feel threatened by a mongoose. But, mongooses move quickly as cobras attack. Their thick skin and fur protect them from a cobra's venom. A mongoose will capture a cobra by sinking its teeth into the back of the snake's neck. The Indian gray mongoose wins the duel!

Mongooses are not the only threat to cobras. Humans hunt king cobras for their meat, skin, and venom. These things are used in food and medicine. Humans also threaten cobra **habitats** through **deforestation**. With fewer places to live, the king cobra population is dropping. This makes it a **vulnerable** species. Now, there are laws in place to protect king cobras from illegal hunting. People are also working to save their habitats.

An Indian gray mongoose attacks a king cobra.

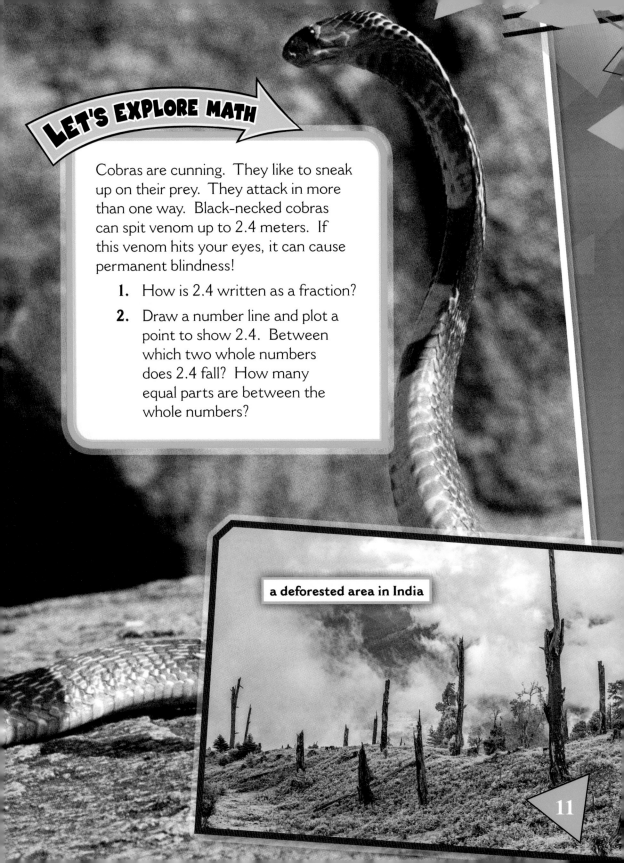

Cobras are cunning. They like to sneak up on their prey. They attack in more than one way. Black-necked cobras can spit venom up to 2.4 meters. If this venom hits your eyes, it can cause permanent blindness!

1. How is 2.4 written as a fraction?

2. Draw a number line and plot a point to show 2.4. Between which two whole numbers does 2.4 fall? How many equal parts are between the whole numbers?

a deforested area in India

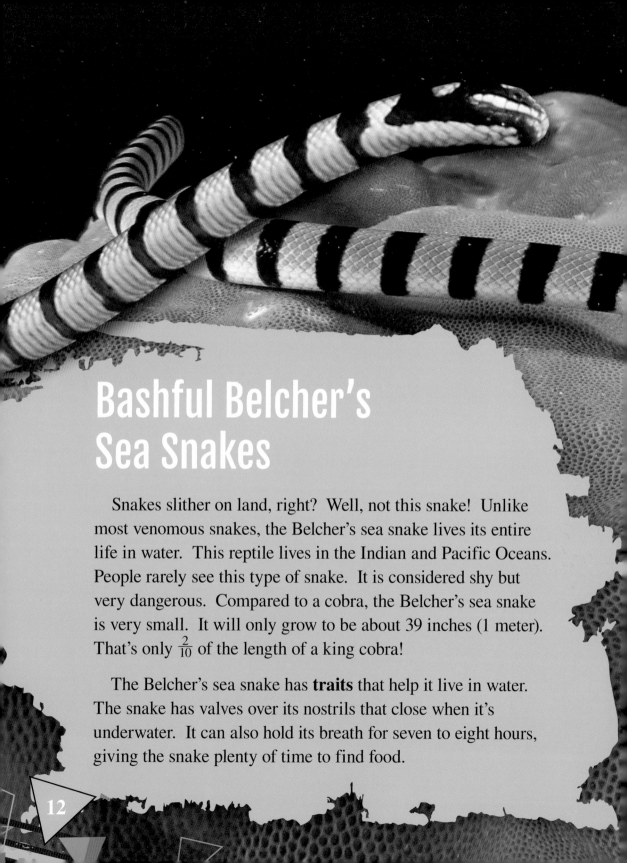

Bashful Belcher's Sea Snakes

Snakes slither on land, right? Well, not this snake! Unlike most venomous snakes, the Belcher's sea snake lives its entire life in water. This reptile lives in the Indian and Pacific Oceans. People rarely see this type of snake. It is considered shy but very dangerous. Compared to a cobra, the Belcher's sea snake is very small. It will only grow to be about 39 inches (1 meter). That's only $\frac{2}{10}$ of the length of a king cobra!

The Belcher's sea snake has **traits** that help it live in water. The snake has valves over its nostrils that close when it's underwater. It can also hold its breath for seven to eight hours, giving the snake plenty of time to find food.

The sea snake spends its whole life in water. Its predators live in the water, too. Large fish like tiger sharks hunt and eat the Belcher's sea snake.

The Belcher's sea snake is one of the most venomous snakes in the world and is considered 100 times more lethal than any other snake. However, the Belcher's sea snake only releases venom $\frac{1}{4}$ of the time it strikes. It takes only $\frac{1}{100}$ of the venom in one bite to kill a human!

Belcher's sea snakes

LET'S EXPLORE MATH

It takes $\frac{1}{100}$ of the venom in a Belcher's sea snake's bite to kill a human. It takes about $\frac{5}{100}$ of the venom in a cobra's bite to kill a human.

1. Use two hundredths grids to show $\frac{1}{100}$ and $\frac{5}{100}$.

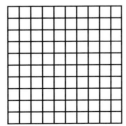 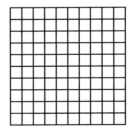

2. Write $\frac{1}{100}$ and $\frac{5}{100}$ as decimals. Compare the decimals using >, <, or =.

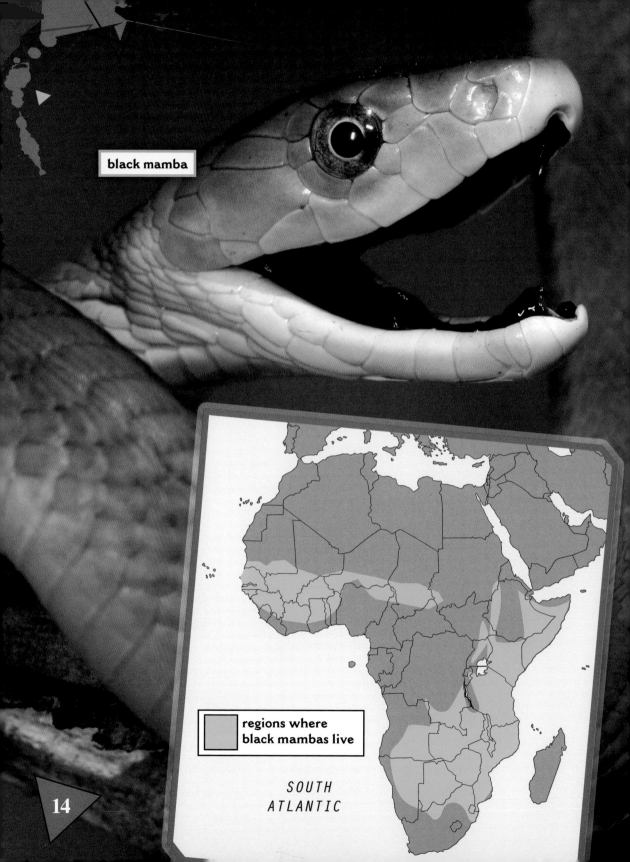

black mamba

regions where
black mambas live

SOUTH
ATLANTIC

Beastly Black Mambas

When people see black mambas for the first time, they are often confused. Their bodies aren't black at all. Their bodies are brown, gray, or green. Their color helps them **camouflage** with their environment. So, where do they get their name? Surprisingly, the name comes from the color inside their mouths. This feature is unique to black mambas.

Barely trailing behind cobras in size, black mambas can grow to be 14 ft. (4 m) long. They are Africa's longest venomous snakes. Like king cobras, these snakes can live up to 20 years.

Black mambas attack when they feel trapped. They will bite several times to defend themselves, even though one bite is enough to cause death. With each bite, they inject enough venom to kill more than 10 people. In fact, only two drops of their venom is enough to make a person's heart stop beating! Without **antivenin**, a victim of a bite only has 20 minutes to live. Many of these victims live in areas that are far from hospitals, which makes the situation even more threatening.

Black mambas might seem scary, but they have their own fears. While black mambas are often found in pairs or small groups, they are no match for predators. Similar to king cobras, mongooses are natural predators of black mambas. Foxes and birds also hunt these venomous snakes. A snake eagle may crush a black mamba with its sharp talons or drop it from high altitudes to kill it. But, the biggest threat to black mambas is humans. People kill black mambas to prevent them from attacking humans.

Capturing a black mamba is not an easy task. It is the fastest land snake in the world. It can travel 12 miles per hour (20 kilometers per hour). That's faster than an average human can run. Black mambas use their speed to escape from danger more than to sneak up on prey. They attack people only when threatened or cornered.

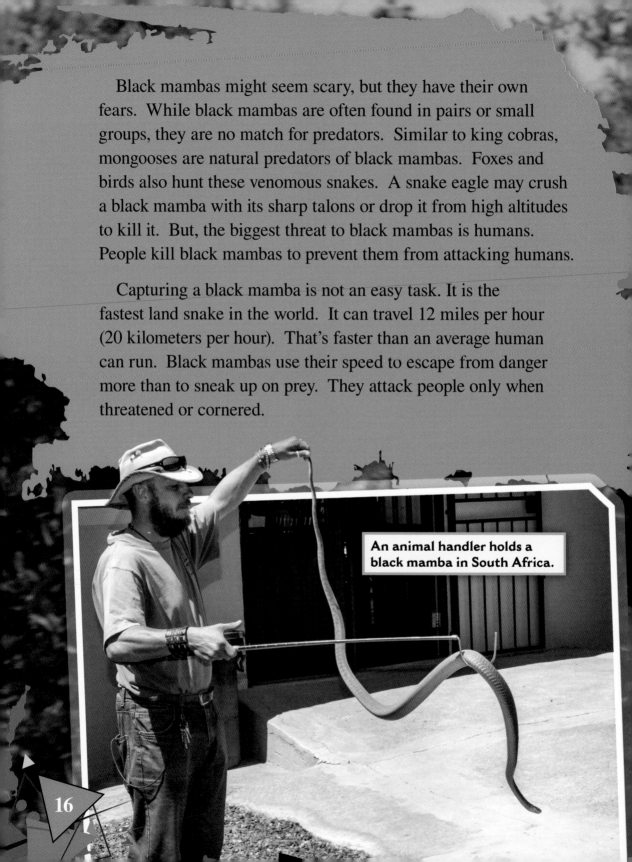

An animal handler holds a black mamba in South Africa.

A brown snake eagle grasps a black mamba in its talons.

A scientist measures the speed of a black mamba. Its speed is 20.31 kilometers per hour.

1. Draw the number line shown below. Use it to plot a point showing 20.31.

    20   20.1   20.2   20.3   20.4   20.5   20.6   20.7   20.8   20.9   30

2. Between which two decimals does 20.31 fall? Which of these decimals is closer to 20.31? How do you know?

Incredible Inland Taipans

If you ever find yourself in Australia, be sure to watch your step! You might run into the inland taipan (TI-pan). Some scientists say it is the world's most venomous snake. Scientists often call it the "fierce snake." It gets this nickname because of its **fatal** venom. It is also famous for the way it attacks its prey. Inland taipans rapidly bite their prey many times, although one bite will most likely do the trick!

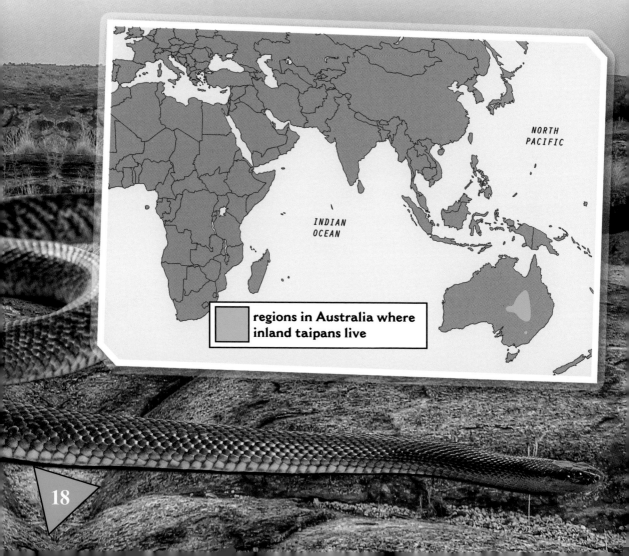

NORTH PACIFIC

INDIAN OCEAN

regions in Australia where inland taipans live

Inland taipans are not colorful snakes. They are typically light yellow or dark brown. These colors act as camouflage that helps them stay out of plain sight. Inland taipans also change color based on seasons. During the summer, the lighter color helps them stay cool. During the winter, the darker color helps them absorb the sun's rays to keep warm. Inland taipans are never too hot or too cold!

inland taipan

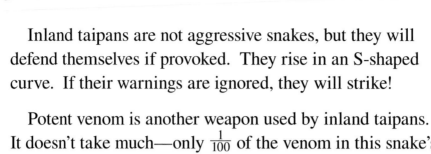

Inland taipans are not aggressive snakes, but they will defend themselves if provoked. They rise in an S-shaped curve. If their warnings are ignored, they will strike!

Potent venom is another weapon used by inland taipans. It doesn't take much—only $\frac{1}{100}$ of the venom in this snake's bite is needed to kill a human. Inland taipan attacks are ferocious. Similar to black mambas, inland taipans strike multiple times in one attack. They bite quickly and accurately, giving prey no time to fight back. They wait patiently for prey to grow still and die. Then, it's time to eat.

inland taipan

Only about $\frac{1}{10}$ of the venom in a black mamba's bite is needed to kill a human. Only about $\frac{1}{100}$ of the venom in an inland taipan's bite is needed to kill a human.

1. Write $\frac{1}{10}$ and $\frac{1}{100}$ as decimals in a place value chart similar to the one below.

hundreds	tens	ones	.	tenths	hundredths
			.		
			.		

2. Use the place value chart and >, <, or = to compare the decimals. Explain your reasoning.

king brown snake

Inland taipans have predators, too. Their main predators are king brown snakes. It is not unusual for snakes to eat other snakes. But, king brown snakes are special because they are **immune** to the venom of inland taipans. This means the venom of inland taipans can't kill king brown snakes.

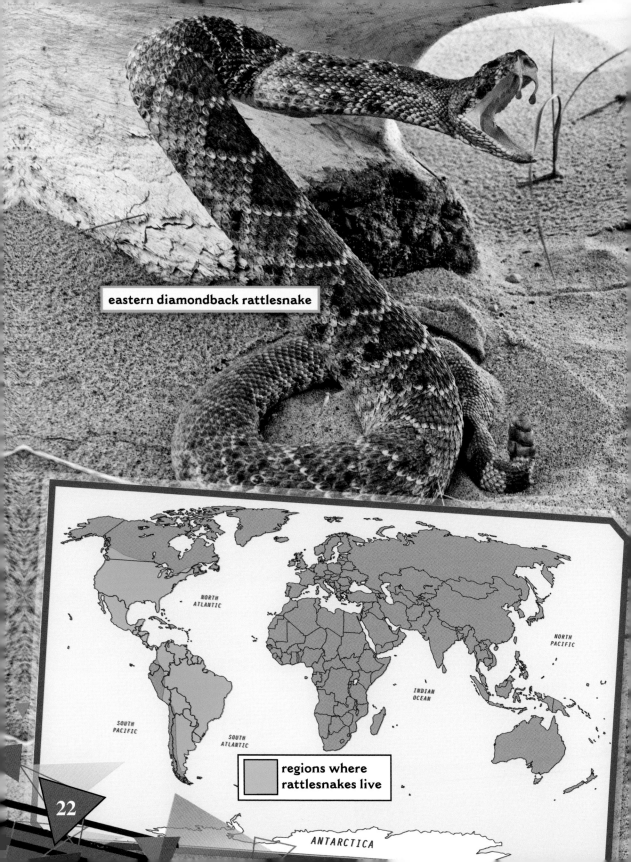

eastern diamondback rattlesnake

regions where rattlesnakes live

NORTH ATLANTIC

NORTH PACIFIC

INDIAN OCEAN

SOUTH PACIFIC

SOUTH ATLANTIC

ANTARCTICA

Reluctant Rattlesnakes

   Next stop: North and South America. All 32 types of rattlesnakes call these continents home. These snakes have adapted to survive in many places. Their habitats include mountains, deserts, and plains. Eastern diamondback rattlesnakes are the largest venomous snake in North America. They can grow to be 8 ft. (2 m) long. They can weigh up to 10 lbs. (5 kg). Their main colors are brown and black so they can blend in. Unlike other snakes, they also have distinct yellow and black diamond shapes along their backs.

   Rattlesnakes have to watch out for predators like kingsnakes. Kingsnakes are immune to rattlesnake venom. They can get close enough to kill a rattlesnake easily. Eagles, hawks, and roadrunners will also attack them. These snakes have to be on the lookout for people, too! Just like black mambas and king cobras, humans are one of the main predators of rattlesnakes.

   A unique trait of adult rattlesnakes is their ability to control the amount of venom in a bite. Scientists think that they do not want to waste venom. They use their venom only $\frac{2}{10}$ of the time they bite. And, less than half of those bites have the power to kill.

What sets rattlesnakes apart from other venomous snakes? You guessed it—their rattles!

The rattle is found on the end of the snake's tail. When a rattlesnake is born, it only has its first rattle segment, or birth button. Each time the snake sheds its skin, it adds another part to the end of its rattle. This makes the rattle longer. It is a **myth**, however, to think that the length of a rattle tells the age of the rattlesnake. Rattles break and pieces fall off all the time. Also, rattlesnakes shed more than once a year. In fact, a baby rattlesnake may shed as early as two weeks after it is born. For these reasons, it is difficult to tell how old a rattlesnake is by simply looking at its rattle.

Rattlesnakes use their rattles to warn potential predators to back away. It sounds similar to a baby's rattle. Interestingly, the rattle is made from keratin, the same material as your fingernails! These snakes don't want to attack people. So if you hear a rattle, back away. You've been warned!

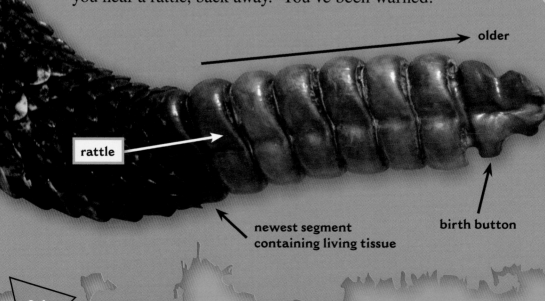

older

rattle

newest segment containing living tissue

birth button

shedded snake skin

A researcher studies the strike speed of two rattlesnakes. She finds that the cottonmouth rattlesnake strikes in 2.9 milliseconds. The Texas rat snake strikes in 2.6 milliseconds.

1. Draw and shade bar models like these to represent 2.9 and 2.6.

2.9

2.6

2. Compare 2.9 and 2.6 using >, <, or =. Explain your reasoning.

Venom: Dangerous but Helpful

Each type of venomous snake has its own unique traits that set it apart from the rest. But, they all definitely have one thing in common: if they feel threatened, they will bite!

There are many myths about what people should do if a venomous snake bites them. But, believing these myths can have deadly results. People should not try to suck the venom out of a bite, put ice on a bite, or take any medicine unless a doctor prescribes it.

There are some important things people should do if they are bitten. They should call 9-1-1 right away. If possible, they should try to identify the snake. Then, they can describe it to a doctor. Finally, they should sit or lie still. This way, the venom doesn't spread through their body as quickly.

A doctor demonstrates snake bite survival skills in Indonesia by wrapping a boy's arm in a bandage.

A scientist extracts venom from a viper.

Snake venom can kill, but it can also be helpful to humans. Venom from a king cobra can help people who are in pain. The venom of a pit viper is used to make medicine to help lower people's blood pressure. Scientists are testing snake venom to find out whether it can help people who have cancer. Most will agree that venomous snakes are dangerous, but people can also benefit from them, too!

⚙ Problem Solving

Suppose you are a **herpetologist,** a scientist who studies snakes. Your job is to create snake displays for a new reptile exhibit at a zoo. The reptile exhibit has 10 cages that are equal in size.

1. Choose four different types of snakes you read about in this book. Draw a model like the one shown. Then, write the name of each snake in one section of the model.

2. What fraction of the model does each type of snake represent? How can this be written as a decimal?

3. What fraction of the whole exhibit do all of the snakes occupy? How can this be written as a decimal?

4. Is more than $\frac{1}{2}$ or less than $\frac{1}{2}$ of the whole exhibit occupied by snakes? Explain your thinking.

Reptile Exhibit

Glossary

adapted—changed so that it is easier to live in a particular place

agility—ability to move quickly and easily

antivenin—remedy used to counteract venom

camouflage—blend into surroundings

continent—a large land mass on Earth

deforestation—the act of cutting down or burning all the trees in an area

fatal—causing death

habitats—places where plants or animals normally live or grow

herpetologist—a scientist who studies snakes

immune—protected from a poison or bacteria

ingest—to swallow or absorb

myth—popular belief that is false

paralyzes—makes incapable of moving

predators—animals that kill and eat other animals

prey—animals that are hunted and killed

traits—qualities that make living things different from one another

venom—poison

venomous—any animal that uses venom as a defense

vulnerable—open to attack

Index

Answer Key

Let's Explore Math

page 7:

page 11:

1. $2.4 = 2\frac{4}{10}$ or $2\frac{2}{5}$

2. Between 2 and 3; 10 equal parts

page 13:

1. 1 part for $\frac{1}{100}$ and 5 parts for $\frac{5}{100}$ should be shaded

2. $\frac{1}{100} = 0.01$; $\frac{5}{100} = 0.05$; $0.01 < 0.05$ or $0.05 > 0.01$

page 17:

1. 20.31 should be labeled slightly to the right of 20.3

2. Between 20.3 and 20.4; 20.31 is closer to 20.3; Answers will vary.

page 21:

1. $\frac{1}{10} = 0.1$; $\frac{1}{100} = 0.01$

2. $0.1 > 0.01$ or $0.01 < 0.1$; 0.1 has more tenths so it is greater than 0.01.

page 25:

1. For 2.9, 2 wholes and 9 of the 10 parts should be shaded. For 2.6, 2 wholes and 6 of the 10 parts should be shaded.

2. $2.9 > 2.6$ or $2.6 < 2.9$; 9 tenths is greater than 6 tenths, so 2.9 is greater than 2.6.

Problem Solving

1. Answers will vary.

2. $\frac{1}{10}$; 0.1

3. $\frac{4}{10}$; 0.4

4. Less than $\frac{1}{2}$; Answers will vary, but should include that $\frac{4}{10} < \frac{5}{10}$ and $\frac{5}{10} = \frac{1}{2}$, so $\frac{4}{10} < \frac{1}{2}$.